MY FIRST ENCYCLOPEDIA

An eye-catching series of information books designed to encourage young children to find out more about the world around them. Each one is carefully prepared by a subject specialist with the help of experienced writers and educational advisers.

KINGFISHER
Kingfisher Publications Plc
New Penderel House, 283-288 High Holborn, London WC1V 7HZ

First published in paperback by Kingfisher Publications Plc 1994
2 4 6 8 10 9 7 5 3 1

1BP/0500/SF/(FR)/135MA

Originally published in hardback under the series title Young World
This edition © copyright Kingfisher Publications Plc 2000
Text & Illustrations © copyright Kingfisher Publications Plc 1992

ISBN 1 85697 268 2

Phototypeset by Waveney Typesetters, Norwich
Printed in China

People and Places

Kingfisher

Author
Dominique Rist

Translator
Pat Pailing

Series consultant
Brian Williams

Editor
Véronique Herbold

Designer
Anne Boyer

Illustrators
Graffito (maps)
Marc Lagarde
Barry Mitchell
Jean-Marc Pau
Etiénne Souppart
Valérie Stetten
Jean Torton

About this book

There are five thousand million people on Earth, and you are one of them! We all share one world, but we are all different. We may wear different clothes, or we may speak different languages and have different customs.

People live in places that look very different from one another. Some countries are dry and scorching hot. Others are wet but just as hot, or cool and damp, or cold and snowy. These differences affect the way people live – the clothes we wear, the food we eat and the homes we build.

This book takes you right around the globe, from the huge continents of America, Europe, Africa, Asia, and Australia to tiny islands in the Pacific Ocean. On the way you'll see people in particular communities – Inuits fishing in the frozen north, children playing on a city street, monks chanting in a mountain monastery, shearers at work on a sheep station. Each community is an important part of our fascinating world.

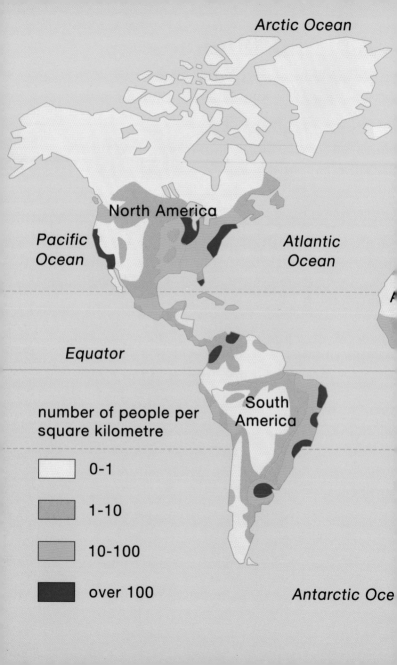

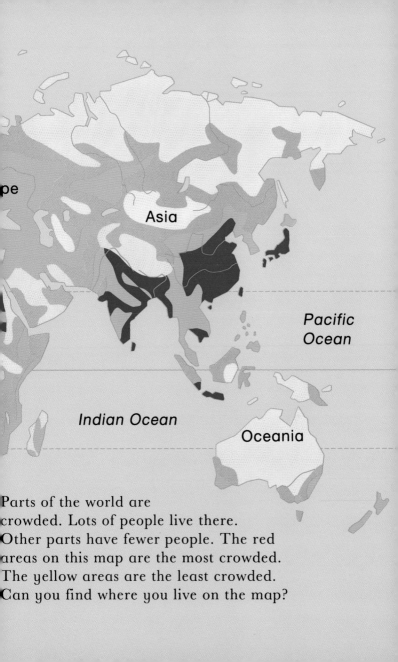

pe

Asia

Pacific
Ocean

Indian Ocean

Oceania

Parts of the world are
crowded. Lots of people live there.
Other parts have fewer people. The red
areas on this map are the most crowded.
The yellow areas are the least crowded.
Can you find where you live on the map?

CONTENTS

PEOPLE EVERYWHERE

"Hello!" 14
Home sweet home 16
Time to eat 18
Going to work 20
Sports 22
Religion 24
On the move 26
Amazing facts 28

AMERICA

The frozen north 30
Land of forests 32
An Indian festival 34
City streets 36
A cattle ranch 38
In the Caribbean 40
A town square 42
Market day 44
Indians of the Amazon 46

Music in Brazil.................. 48
Amazing facts 50

EUROPE
In Scandinavia.................. 52
A fishing village 54
A city in Europe............... 56
Farming in Europe........... 58
A mountain village........... 60
In Spain.......................... 62
Islands in the sun 64
A gypsy festival............... 66
Amazing facts 68

AFRICA
Going to market.............. 70
Desert travellers............... 72
Beside the River Nile 74
A town in Africa 76
Village life 78
Life on the water.............. 80
Farming in Africa 82
An ostrich farm............... 84
Amazing facts 86

ASIA

On a kibbutz..................88
Oil in the desert..............90
In Afghanistan................92
Among the Mongols.........94
China, Asia's giant..........96
A monastery...................98
A holy river...................100
The rice growers...........102
Gifts for the gods..........104
In Japan.......................106
People of Papua............108
Amazing facts...............110

OCEANIA

A sheep farm.................112
People of the outback.....114
In New Zealand............116
Polynesian islanders.......118
Amazing facts...............120

INDEX 121

People
everywhere

Hello!

السَّلامُ عَلَيْكُم

jamm nga fënaan

BONJOUR!

تابق

မင်္ဂလာပါ။

নমস্কার

There are almost three thousand language
in the world. Many people speak more tha
one language.

14

Buenos días

здра́вствуй

שָׁלוֹם, בֹּקֶר טוֹב

ਸਤ ਸ੍ਰੀ ਅਕਾਲ

aydın

καλημέρα

안녕

おはよう

The words people speak and write may
sound and look very different. Here is how
to say "hello" in just a few languages.

Home sweet home

Arctic igloo

Indian tepee

Tuareg te

Australian house

Borneo
longhouse

Benir
stilt hou

cave
dwelling

Irish
cottage

Spanis
hacienc

eople live in many kinds of homes, built of
any kinds of materials, on the ground and
n water.

golian yurt

mobile home

Chinese sampan

Southern
African
hut

rsh Arab
w house

Mali mud house

iterranean
house

Venetian
palace

skyscraper

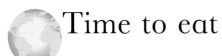 # Time to eat

People eat different kinds of food

Everyone gathers round in Arab countries,

You kneel on cushions in Japan,

n different places.

nd in Africa.

nd sit round a table in France.

19

bringing
the news

looking after people

entertaining people

ll over the world, the same jobs have to
e done.

nding and cooking food

uilding bridges and tunnels

21

Sports

running

jumping

weight-lifting

basketball

tennis

American footba

surfing

skiing

All over the world people enjoy playing and watching sport.

gymnastics   ice-skating   swimming

umo wrestling   boxing

motor racing   horse racing

Religion

Christians believe in one God and in Jesus Christ. They worship in churches.

Jews believe in one God and in the Messiah. The Wailing Wall in Jerusalem is an important place of prayer.

Muslims believe in one God, Allah. Their religion is called Islam. Muslims go on pilgrimage to Mecca.

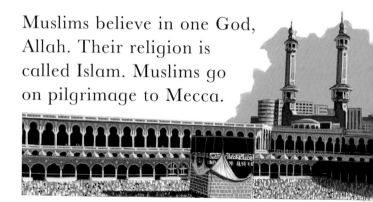

Hindu pilgrims visit the holy city of Varanasi. Hindus worship many gods, such as Brahma, Shiva and Vishnu.

Buddhists follow the teachings of Gautama, the Buddha. There are statues of him in Buddhist temples.

Shinto is the ancient religion of Japan. Shinto means "way of the gods" in Japanese. People worship many gods in Shinto shrines.

25

On the move

People travel all over the world,

They take a train, or a bus,

They cross the sea by plane,

n foot and on horseback, even by camel.

nd they ride in a jeep or on a bike.

r in a boat.

Amazing facts

Every year there are millions more people in the world. In 1950 there were 2,500 million people. Today there are more than twice that number.

Almost half the people of the world live in towns and cities.

All over the world, women usually live longer than men.

There are 189 countries in the world. Each country has its own government, flag, capital city and money.

The biggest country in the world is Russia. It covers more than 17 million square kilometres.

America

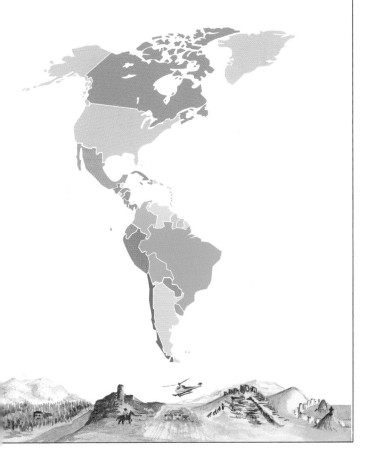

The frozen north

The far north of Canada is one of the coldest places on Earth. This is where the Inuits live.

Everyone wears warm clothes to keep out the icy cold. Planes bring food and other supplies for the winter.

Sledges pulled by dogs are a good way to get around. But people also drive skidoos.

Rubbing noses is the Inuit way of kissing.

his man is fishing through a hole
the ice. Close by is the
loo he has built for
elter from the cold.
lthough the igloo
made of ice,
is warm inside.
uits use the
loos only when
ey go fishing in
e winter.

31

Land of forests

Vast forests stretch across Canada, which is the second biggest country in the world. The forests supply trees for timber.

Lumberjacks cut down the trees with chainsaws. Logging trucks haul the trees to the sawmills, to be cut into planks of timbe

eople in Canada and the United States
ve to eat maple syrup in cakes or on
ancakes. The syrup comes from maple
ees. At the end of winter, snow still covers
e ground. The maple trees have no leaves.
ow is the time to drill holes in the tree
unk. The watery sap inside the tree drips
ut into a bucket. Then the sap is carried to
cabin called the sugarhouse, and boiled.
turns into a sticky, sweet syrup. Delicious!

33

An Indian festival

The Indians were the first people to live in America. They still celebrate their ancient festivals. These Pueblo Indians of the United States are dancing to celebrate the Maize Festival.

The dancers wear special costumes and wear corn cobs on their heads. They sing to make the rain fall and bring them a good harvest.

When Pueblo children play with wooden kachina dolls, they learn about Indian history and legends. Each doll is painted to represent a magical spirit of the earth, sky or water. This is a winged spirit doll. It represents a spirit of the sky.

This Pueblo medicine man is trying to heal someone who is ill. He draws signs in the sand. His helpers chant songs.

City streets

The United States of America is home to many people whose parents, grandparents, great grandparents or great-great grandparents came from other countries.

Many Americans live in big cities. These children play basketball in the street. Perhaps they dream of becoming sports stars one day.

kyscrapers are the tallest buildings in the
orld. They tower above the busy streets.

A cattle ranch

As well as cities, there are wide open spaces in the United States. American farmers raise cattle on big farms called ranches. Cowboys look after the cattle.

This cowboy uses a rope called a lasso to catch a stray from the herd. He is an exper rider, and his horse is well trained to gallo and twist and turn.

fter a long, tiring day on horseback, the
>wboys relax around a campfire.

hese children
~e helping to
ok after the
1by animals.

ome farms are so big that farmers use
:licopters as well as horses and jeeps.
uge combine harvesters cut the wheat.

39

In the Caribbean

harvesting
bananas

The people of the
Caribbean live on island
known as the West Indie
It is warm all year roun
with lots of sunshine.
Tourists visit the islands.
to enjoy the beaches and
the mountain scenery.

Many of the islanders are fishermen. They
go out in small boats and catch fish in the
warm waters around the islands. When they
return with their catch, they pull their boats
up onto the beach near the village and sell
their fish. Later they spread out their nets to
dry. This fisherman is mending his nets in
the shade of a coconut palm.

A town square

It is noon, the hottest part of the day so the square is almost empty. The people of this small town in Mexico are taking a break from work. They rest in the cool shade under the arches. It is pleasant to eat in the open air – a plate of tasty beans with pancakes called tortillas, or sweetcorn roasted on the cob.

Every town has its own fiesta or festival once a year. Then people fill the square.

During the fiesta, there are fireworks and music and dancing. Children try to break open a pot called the piñata, to get the sweets inside.

Market day

The people of the Andes Mountains live in one of the highest places in the world. Only the Himalayas in Asia are higher. It can be cold in the mountains so people wear clothes made from sheep and llama wool which is dyed in bright colours

On market day everyone comes to town. Women carry their babies in shawls tied round their shoulders. People from the mountain farms come in trucks or on foot with their animals. They bring vegetables such as beans, yams and potatoes to sell in the street. They buy cooking pots and tools to take home.

Indians of the Amazon

The Amazon Indians live in the
biggest rainforest in the world. It is hot an
wet, and the forest is very thick. There are
hardly any roads. People live in villages in
small clearings. They grow vegetables, and
the forest supplies them with everything
else they need.

The Amazon Indians go into the forest to
gather fruit, to hunt animals and to catch
fish in the rivers.

unters go off into the
rest for a day or so.
his man is hunting
h with a bow and
row.

hildren help too.
hey look after babies and gather food.

Music in Brazil

Much of the Amazon forest is in Brazil, the biggest country in South America. But most Brazilians live in cities. There is a famous carnival every year in the city of Rio de Janeiro. People come out into the streets and dance to the music.

here are bands playing in the street all
ear round. These drummers play tall
frican drums called bongos and old oil-
rums called batucadas. Two men are
ancing to the music.

Amazing facts

Christopher Columbus sailed from Spain t
the Caribbean in 1492. He called the
people of this 'New World' Indians, becau
he thought he had reached the East Indies
of Asia.

After Columbus' voyage, many people fro
Spain came to Mexico. Mexicans still spea
Spanish. Brazilians speak Portuguese
because most of the people who came to
Brazil were from Portugal.

Mexico City is the most crowded city in th
world. More than 20 million people live
there.

The tallest building in the world is in
America. It is the Sears Tower in Chicago

The maple leaf is the national symbol of
Canada. It appears on Canada's flag.

Europe

In Scandinavia

Far up in the North are the Scandinavian countries of Finland, Sweden and Norway.

Scandinavia has cold, snowy winters. Ice covers the lakes and ponds. Sometimes the sea freezes over too. So people drill holes i the ice when they go fishing. They get out their sledges and skates. Hundreds of peop take part in cross-country ski races.

mmers are warmer. Holiday-makers drive
it of town to the lakes and forests. They
ke hot steam baths called saunas inside a
ooden cabin. To cool off, they go
/imming in the lake.

A fishing village

On the edge of the Atlantic Ocean, fishing has always been important. These pictures show a fishing community in Brittany, which is a region of France. The fishermen go out to sea in large boats called trawlers.

The trawlers drag nets through the water catch sole, sardines and tuna. The fishermen pack the fish in boxes, with ice t keep them fresh. They stay at sea for seve days. Then they return to their home port

he boxes of fish are unloaded and sold in
e fish market. Tourists on holiday come to
atch.

he people of
rittany are called
retons. Some
reton women still
ake and wear the
aditional costume
ith lace caps.

A city in Europe

Most of the people of Europe live an work in towns and cities. Some European towns are small. Others have grown over many years into big cities.

There are public gardens and parks for everyone to enjoy. Sometimes a band com to play on the bandstand.

The centre of the city is often the business area, with offices, banks and shops. Side b side, buildings old and new tell the history of the city.

isitors and townspeople can
ave a drink and a meal at
café in the square.

the weather is fine, it's fun to sit and
atch the world pass by.

Farming in Europe

On a small farm in Poland, everyone gets up early to help. There are fields to plough, crops to plant and pick, cows to milk and chickens to feed.

Farming is hard work. On the large farms, farmers use machines to help get the work done more quickly.

_..._rope's farmers grow a lot of wheat. They _..._e combine harvesters to gather in the crop _..._ harvest time, towards the end of summer.

_..._hen they use _..._ctors to plough _..._e fields and sow _..._ore wheat.

_..._rmers also keep cattle, for milk and meat. _..._me of the milk is made into butter, _..._eam, yoghurt and cheese.

A mountain village

The Alps are Europe's most famous mountains. In winter they are covered with snow. This mountain village in Switzerland becomes crowded. It is the skiing season. People come to the Alps on skiing holidays. They take a ski lift up the mountain, and then they ski down.

In summer, much of the snow melts and the skiers have gone.

ow cows can
aze in green
ustures high
n the Alps.
hey give rich
ilk. Bees find
ollen in the
eadow flowers and
ake honey in their hives.

The skiers will be back with
the snow next winter.

In Spain

Some parts of Europe have much warmer climates than others. In Spain and other countries in the south, it is warm enough t grow grapes. The grapes ripen in the hot summer sun. In September they are ready to be harvested.

ow the workers cut bunches
grapes from the vines and
ad them into baskets. The
apes are taken to a press
d made into wine. At the
d of a good harvest, the
ape growers and the
nemakers all celebrate
gether with a feast.

Islands in the sun

For a warm, sunny holiday, many Europeans go to Greece and its islands.

Some of the islanders make their living by fishing from small boats.

In summer, the days are long and hot. People are glad of the shade in narrow streets. They sit and talk at tables outside small cafés.

Because there is so much heat and very little rain, much of the land is dry. But farmers grow good crops of olives and walnuts. They also keep goats and sheep. A donkey is useful for carrying small loads.

A gypsy festival

Gypsies have travelled around Europe for hundreds of years. Once they lived in caravans pulled by horses. Now most gypsies have motor homes. But they still love horses. And many still speak the old gypsy language called Romany.

Every May, gypsies gather from all over Europe for a great religious festival.

The festival is held in Saintes-Maries de la Mer, in the South of France. For two days, people sing and dance and play music together. A procession goes to the seashore to bathe two statues of saints.

Amazing facts

The biggest city in Europe is Moscow, Russia's capital city.

Europe's most watery city is Venice in Ital[...] Venice is built on the edge of the sea. It h[...] more canals than streets, so people often travel about in boats instead of cars and buses.

Europe is the second smallest of the Earth'[...] continents. Yet only Asia has more people.

Twelve countries belong to the European Union or European Community. Other countries are waiting to join.

Africa

Going to market

In North Africa, in the country of Morocco, the old part of town is called the medina. People going to market pass through a large gateway into the medina.

They come to buy food, jewellery, pots and carpets. Each trade has its own market in its own street, called the souk.

This man is a tanner or leatherworker. He soaks animal skins in dye to colour them. Other people use the leather to make bags and shoes to sell.

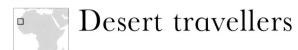

Desert travellers

The Sahara is one of the hottest plac[es] to live. The Tuareg are nomads who wand[er] the desert with their camels and goats.

They live in tents which they can pack up and load onto their camels.

The Tuareg set off with their camels in a
caravan, with one camel following another.
A camel driver leads the
caravan across the desert. He
knows the best way to the
next stopping place. At night,
he finds the way by looking
at the stars.

It hardly ever rains in the
Sahara. Camels can go
for days without water,
but people need water
every day.

So the Tuareg fetch water from wells and
carry it with them in goatskin containers.

Beside the River Nile

The Nile is Africa's longest river. It flows right through Egypt. Egypt's farmers grow wheat and vegetables in fields beside the river. Without water from the Nile, the land would be a desert like the Sahara.

armers dig irrigation canals and ditches to carry the Nile's water to their crops. Day and night, oxen turn the waterwheels that keep the water flowing.

Sailing boats called feluccas carry people and goods up and down the Nile.

A town in Africa

Towns begin as places where people meet to trade. Many of the large African towns are ports near the sea or by a river. So boats are just as useful as trucks.

Africa's towns are growing quickly. Some are now gre cities, with tall skyscrapers.

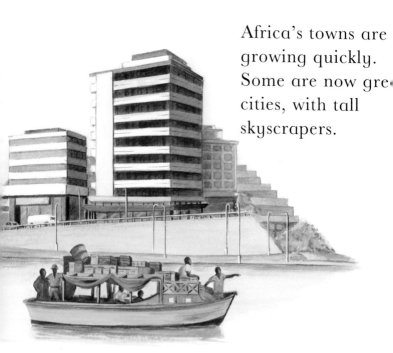

More and more people are leaving countr villages to live in towns. They go to find jobs in offices, shops and factories.

the city of Dakar in West Africa, these
ople are shopping in an open-air market.
aders set out vegetables and spices, cloth
d other goods on the ground. There is
endly arguing over prices. Women often
rry shopping home on their heads.

Village life

Villages in Africa can look very different from one another because people use different materials and build in differe ways. The houses in this village on the Ivory Coast have thatched roofs.

The people of the village enjoy stories, gossip and games. Beneath a baobab tree, men are playing a game called awale. The two players move seeds around holes in a block of wood.

The women are preparing a meal together. They pound millet or cassava into flour for baking bread.

Some of the villagers are spinning cotton and weaving it into cloth on a loom.

Life on the water

This is a fishing village in on the coast of Benin in West Africa. The houses are built on stilts high above the water. There are n streets, and people move about in small boats. The men go out fishing every morning. They throw out their nets and pu in the catch.

ter a morning's fishing, the men paddle
ir boats back to the village. The women
ld a floating market. They sell the fresh
h brought back in the boats. They buy
it and vegetables brought out from the
ore by traders.

Farming in Africa

In Central Africa, farmers grow rows
and rows of tea bushes on the hillsides.
These workers in Zaire carefully pick the
best leaves from the bushes. The leaves are
dried and crumbled, and shipped all over
the world. They end up in the tea bags we
use to make tea.

Farmers also grow coffee beans in Central
and East Africa.

In the forests
of Africa,
bridges across
the rivers are
made of lianas
or creepers.
You need a good
head for heights to
cross this swaying
bridge! It hangs from
trees on each side of
the river.

The River Congo flows through the vast
rainforest of Zaire, to the Atlantic Ocean.

An ostrich farm

A very unusual kind of farm is found in South Africa. It is an ostrich farm! Ostriches are the biggest birds in the world. The males have magnificent feathers.

Ostriches cannot fly but they have powerful legs, so they can run fast and they are very strong. They can even carry people on their backs for a short distance. But watch out when an ostrich kicks!

Tourists come to ostrich farms to see the birds.

eepers look after the flocks of ostriches on
e farm. The female ostriches lay their
ge eggs inside special shelters. One
trich can lay as many as ten eggs.
o other bird lays
ch large eggs.

hen the chicks
tch, they soon run
fast as their
rents.

Amazing facts

People lived in Africa over two million years ago. Now scientists have found the bones and footprints of even older human-like beings.

The Sahara was not always a sandy desert. It once had rivers and grasslands, and hippos and giraffes lived there.

Cairo in Egypt is Africa's biggest city. More than six million people live there.

Almost 700 million people live in Africa. There are 52 countries, and more than 800 different languages.

Asia

On a kibbutz

These children live in Israel. Their home is a farm called a kibbutz. They all live together as one large family.

veryone works together
n the kibbutz.
he farmers
ave turned
ry land into
reen fields and
rchards. They
row vegetables
nd fruit for
le abroad.

hese workers are picking oranges and
utting them into crates.

Oil in the desert

Saudi Arabia is a hot, dry place. Bedouin and other nomads cross the Arabian Desert on their camels. Beneath the sand there is oil. Engineers drill wells deep underground to reach the oil. Then road tankers and pipes carry the oil to ships waiting at the coast. The Arab countries sell their oil to the rest of the world.

In town and in the desert, men wear loose robes and a head-dress called a keffiyah. Most of the women wear a veil.

n the desert and up in the mountains,
eople hunt with falcons and dogs, just as
eir ancestors did. This man holds the
lcon on his wrist, and at the right moment
e launches the bird towards its prey.

In Afghanistan

Afghanistan has deserts, mountains, and pla

In the plains to the north, Afghan horsemen play an exciting game called bozkashi. The ball is a blown-up goatskin. One rider grabs it and carries it. The other players try to take it from him.

A covered market or bazaar is sheltered from the summer sun and the winter snow. People come to the bazaar from far-off mountain villages to buy and sell goods.

93

Among the Mongols

The nomads of Mongolia wander the grassy plains with their sheep, goats, cattle, camels and horses. They carry their home with them. A Mongol family's home is a tent called a yurt. It is built with wooden poles and covered with felt cloth. The felt made of wool from the family's animals.

The felt keeps out sun, wind and rain. So a yurt is cool in summer and warm in winter.

his Mongol family prepare
meal inside their yurt.
hen it is time to move on,
ey will take apart the
rt, roll it all up and take
with them.

Mongol children learn
to ride when they are
toddlers. They become
excellent horsemen.

he old Mongol way of life is changing.
any Mongols are no longer nomads. They
ay in one place, on farms or in towns. But
ten they still live in a yurt.

China, Asia's giant

To the south of Mongolia lies China, the giant of Asia. China has more people than any other country in the world.

Many Chinese start the day by doing tai-chi exercises. Then they go off to work, on foot or by bike. In the busy streets people are selling snacks and vegetables, playing chess and mah-jong and reading the news.

A monastery

The world's highest mountains a
in the Himalayas. On the slop
of the mountains are monaster
where monks follow t
teachings of Buddh
They pray and th
study, far from t
noise and crow
of city li

In the country
Bhutan, sor
boys train to
monks from sev
years of ag
They wear simp
robes of yellow
orange. They learn t
prayers and holy chants, a
they watch the religio
ceremonic

A holy river

The River Ganges is the greate
river in India. Hindus belie
it is a holy river. On its ban
are Hindu temples. Peop
visit the city of Varan
to bathe in the Gange

owds of Hindu
lgrims gather at
wn on the steps
ading down to
e Ganges. They
the in the river
 make them-
lves pure. They
ay, and drink a
outhful of water.

Cows wander
about the streets
of Indian cities.
Hindus believe
that cows are
sacred animals.
People do not
harm them.

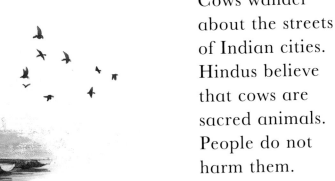

eligion is important in India. There are
stivals and holidays throughout the year.
ot all the people of India are Hindus.
here are also Muslims, Sikhs, Jains
d Christians.

The rice growers

All over Southeast Asia people grow and eat a lot of rice. Rice is a kind of grass. It needs warmth and lots of water to grow well. Farmers plough the fields, and then flood them with water from a canal or a river. Buffalo are better than tractors for this kind of farming.

n this farm in
hailand, rice plants
e carefully grown
om seed in special
ursery fields. Then
ey are planted out
flooded fields
alled paddy fields.

fter three months,
e rice is ready to
arvest. The field is
ained dry. The
armers cut the stems
nd store the rice
rains in granaries.

Gifts for the gods

Bali is one of the many islands of Indonesi
These women offer gifts to the gods, so tha
the gods will protect their villages and
homes, and bring them good luck. They
carry on their heads gifts of rice, fruit and
flowers. Children join in the procession.

he Balinese love
ncing. They start
hen they are very
ung. At the age of
n, girls can dance in
e ceremonies. But it
kes years to learn
l the dance
ovements.

105

In Japan

About 120 million people live on the islands of Japan. Indoors, the Japanese take off their shoes. The floor is covered with tatamis, which are mats made of plaited rice straw.

At mealtime the family kneels around the table.

In the morning, everyone rolls up their futon, or mattress bed, and puts it away.

karate

kendo

judo

The Japanese are good at martial arts.
In kendo, two people fight with staves.
They wear helmets to protect themselves.
In karate and judo, they fight with bare hands and feet.
During the children's festival on 5th May, kites shaped like fish fly high in the sky.

carp kites

calligraphy

School children learn calligraphy, the art of writing with a brush and ink on a long scroll of paper.

People of Papua

Papua New Guinea is a land of mountains and forests. The people are called Papuans. For important feasts, Papuan men paint their faces and wear necklaces of pigs' teeth.

The Papuans live in large villages, in houses made from woven reeds.

They keep pigs and chickens and they look after vegetable gardens.

They grow sweet potatoes, yams and taro. They also harvest bananas and coconuts.

he men hunt and fish. They make their
ws and arrows from split bamboo and
arpened stones. They also carve axe
ads from stones, to sell to tourists. Boys
d girls learn their parents' skills by
lping them. Some children go to school,
t others live in remote mountain areas
th no roads or schools.

ore than 700 different languages are
oken in Papua New Guinea.

Amazing facts

Asia is the biggest of all the continents. Six out of every ten people in the world live in Asia.

China has more than 1,100 million people. That's more than any other country. Next comes India, with about 850 million people.

The world's highest mountain, Mount Everest, is in Asia, in the Himalayas.

Indonesia in Southeast Asia is a country made up of more than 13,000 islands.

The biggest city in Asia is Tokyo, the capital of Japan.

New Guinea is the second biggest island in the world. Only Greenland is bigger.

Oceania

A sheep farm

Australia has some of the biggest farms in the world. The sheep stations are so big that farmers use planes, trucks, motorbikes and horses to get around. At shearing time, the sheep are rounded up into sheds to have their wool cut off.

Cattle stations have huge herds of cattle.

his farm is far from e nearest town and hool. So the farm ildren have lessons home. They listen their teacher over e radio.

someone is ill, the flying doctor comes out the farm by plane.

113

People of the outback

Australia is the home of the Aborigines. They were the first people to live there. Nowadays many Aborigines liv in towns or work on farms.

Other Aborigines still live in the dry wilderness called the outback.

borigines can find
od and water even
a desert. They
nt kangaroos and
her animals with
ears. They also
nt with curved
oomerangs
hich they carve
om wood.

kangaroo

his artist paints the animals of the outback
nd the old Aboriginal legends. He paints
ith coloured earths and burnt wood, on a
ece of bark from the eucalyptus tree.

115

In New Zealand

In the Pacific Ocean to the east of Australia lies New Zealand. It has two ma[in] islands and thousands of smaller ones. So the sea is never far away, even when you live in a city. It's fun to go out in a yacht or a motor boat.

p in the
ountains, the
orth Island is
mous for its
olcanic mud
ools and hot
rings called
ysers.

ew Zealanders are keen on sport,
pecially rugby, cricket and bowls.
ople meet at this bowls
ub for a game
d a chat.

Polynesian islanders

Scattered across the Pacific Ocean are the tiny islands of Polynesia. The islanders live in villages beside the sea. They go fishing canoes. They beat the water with their paddles to make the fish rise to the surface Then they catch them with spears.

Tall coconut palms gro everywhere. Coconuts a good to eat, with a mil drink inside. The n also gives coconut o The hairy fib around the nut cc be made into rop And the tree trunk cc be hollowed out and made in a canoe. What a useful plan

the clear waters of the coral reef,
swimmers find colourful fish and shells.

's all part of our beautiful world.

Amazing facts

Australia is the only country which is also continent.

Australia has the world's biggest coral reef the Great Barrier Reef. The reef is more than 2,000 kilometres long.

Australia and New Zealand are part of the huge region called Oceania, in the Pacific Ocean. Oceania has thousands of other islands, some of them very small. The islan of Nauru covers an area of just 21 square kilometres.

People came to the Pacific islands from As thousands of years ago. The Maoris were the first people to live in New Zealand.

‍borigines 114-115
‍ghanistan 92-93
‍rica 9, 18, 70-86
‍nazon 46, 48
‍nerica 30-50
‍orth 8, 30-43, 50
‍outh 8, 44-49, 50
‍ndes 44-45
‍ntarctic Ocean 9
‍abian Desert 90-91
‍ctic Ocean 8
‍ia 9, 44, 50, 88-110
‍lantic Ocean 9, 54,
  83
‍stralia 9, 112-115,
  116, 120
‍vale 79

‍ali 104-105
‍obob 79
‍sketball 22, 36
‍tucada 49
‍zaar 93
‍douin 90
‍utan 98
‍ngo 49

boomerang 115
bowls 117
bozkashi 93
Brazil 48-49, 50
bridge 21, 83
Brittany 54-55
Buddhist 25, 98
buffalo 102

Cairo 86
calligraphy 107
camel 27, 72-73, 90,
  94
canal 68, 75, 102
Canada 30-33, 50
canoe 118
caravan 73
Caribbean 40-41, 50
carnival 48
cattle 38-39, 94, 112
chess 96
Chicago 50
children's festival 107
China 96-97, 110
Christian 24, 101
church 24

city 25, 28, 36-37, 48, 50, 56-57, 68, 76-77, 86, 98, 100, 101
coconut 41, 108, 118
Columbus, Christopher 50
Congo 83
continent 68, 110, 120
coral reef 119, 120
cow 58, 61, 101
cowboy 38-39

Dakar 77
dancing 34, 43, 49, 67, 105
desert 72-73, 74, 86, 90-91, 92, 115
doctor 113
donkey 65

Egypt 74-75, 86
Eskimo 30-31
eucalyptus 115
Europe 9, 52-68
Everest 110

Falcon 91
farming 38-39, 45, 58-59, 65, 74, 82, 84-85, 88-89, 95, 102-103, 112-113, 114
felucca 75
festival 34, 43, 66-67, 101, 107
fiesta 43
Finland 52
fishing 31, 41, 47, 54-55, 64, 109, 118
flag 28, 50
flying doctor 113
food 18-19, 21, 30, 70, 115
forest 32-33, 46-47, 48, 53, 83, 108
France 19, 54-55, 66-67
futon 106

Ganges 100-101
geyser 117
goat 65, 72, 94
grape 62-63
Great Barrier Reef 120
Greece 64-65
Greenland 110
gypsy 66-67

imalayas 44, 98, 110
ndu 25, 100-101
me 16-17, 94, 104
rse 27, 38, 39, 66,
94, 112
use 16-17, 76, 108
nting 47, 91, 109,

oo 16, 31
dia 100-101, 110
dian
    Amazon 46-47
    Pueblo 34-35
dian Ocean 9
donesia 104-105, 110
uit 30-31
am 24
and 40-41, 64, 104,
106, 110, 116-119, 120
ael 88-89
ly 68

ain 101
pan 18, 25, 106-107
rusalem 24
w 24
do 107

Kachina doll 35
kangaroo 115
karate 107
keffiyah 90
kendo 107
kibbutz 88-89
kite 107

Language 14-15, 66,
    86, 109
llama 44
lumberjack 32

Maize 34, 45
maize festival 34
Maori 120
maple 33, 50
market 44-45, 55, 70-
    71, 77, 93
martial arts 107
Mecca 24
medicine man 35
medina 70-71
Mexico 42-43, 50
milk 59, 61
monastery 98
Mongolia 94-95, 96

Morocco 70-71
Moscow 68
mountain 44, 60-61, 91,
    92, 93, 98, 108, 110, 117
Mount Everest 110
music 43, 48-49, 67
Muslim 22

Nauru 120
New Guinea 110
news 20, 96
New Zealand 116-117,
    120
Nile 74-75
nomad 72, 90, 94-95
Norway 52

Ocean 8-9, 54, 83
Oceania 112-120
oil 90
ostrich 84-85
outback 114
oxen 75

Pacific Ocean 8, 9,
    116, 118, 120

Papua New Guinea 108
pilgrim 25, 101
pinata 43
plain 93, 94
Poland 58
Polynesia 118-119, 120
port 54, 76
Portugal 50
Pueblo 34-35

Rainforest 46, 83
ranch 38-39
religion 24-25
rice 102-103, 106
Rio de Janeiro 48
river 47, 74-75, 76, 83,
    100-101, 102
road 46, 209
Russia 28, 68

Sahara 72-73, 74, 76
Saintes-Mairies de la
    Mer 66-67
sauna 53
Scandinavia 52-53
school 107, 109, 113
sea 52, 54, 76, 116, 118

ep 44, 65, 94, 112-113
nto 25
ine 25
h 101
ging 34, 35, 67
doo 30
ng 22, 52, 60-61
scraper 37, 76
dge 26, 30, 52
uk 70
uth Africa 84-85
utheast Asia 102, 110
ain 50, 62-63
rt 22-23, 36, 117
eden 52
itzerland 60

i-chi 96
ner 70
ami 106
  82
nple 25, 100
t 16, 72, 94
iiland 103
rist 40, 55, 84, 109
n 28, 42-43, 56, 70,
  6, 90, 95, 113, 114
tor 59, 102

trawler 54
Tuareg 72-73

United States 33, 34,
  36-39, 40

Varanasi 25, 100-101
Venice 68
village 41, 46, 60, 76,
  78-79, 93, 104, 108,
  118

Water 73, 74-75, 102,
  115
well 73
West Indies 40-41
wheat 39, 59, 63, 74
wine 62-63
wool 44, 94, 112
writing 15, 107

Yurt 17, 94-95

Zaire 82-83